A Training Manual

BATTLE OPERATIONS OCCUPANCY TRAINING

BOOT CAMP
FOR CHRISTIANS

2 Timothy 2:4
No man that warreth entangleth himself with the affairs of this life; that he may please him who hath chosen him to be a soldier.

G. WAYNE PARKER

BOOT CAMP FOR CHRISTIANS

Copyright © 2013 by G. Wayne Parker
Published by G. Wayne Parker
www.gwayneparker@verizon.net

Cover design and graphics
by G. Wayne Parker

All rights are reserved. No portion of this book
may be used or reproduced in any format
without written permission of the publisher.

ISBN: 978-0-9911831-0-4

First Edition
2013

Printed in the United States of America

A LOVING ACKNOWLEDGMENT

My very special thanks to Edna, my wonderful wife of thirty years. Truly, a gift from the Lord. She is not only a great wife, she is my best friend next to God. She is my helper, my proof reader, and my partner-soldier in spiritual warfare. Thanks Pud-din!

Contents

Foreword 1

Welcome To Boot Camp 3

Recruitment .... Chapter 1 7

Enlistment .... Chapter 2 11

The Bus Ride In .... Chapter 3 15

Analogy Of The Bus Ride .... Chapter 4 21

Battle .... Chapter 5 25

Operations .... Chapter 6 31

Occupancy .... Chapter 7 39

Training .... Chapter 8 43

Code Of Conduct .... Chapter 9 53

Uniform .... Chapter 10 59

Weapons .... Chapter 11 65

Job Assignment .... Chapter 12 71

Duty Station .... Chapter 13 79

Tour Of Duty .... Chapter 14 85

Biblical Glossary Of Fighting Words 91

Forword

My life was not a life filled with tragedies. I was one that loved having fun filled parties. For the most part life seemed to be exciting. While attending college I decided I would join the Armed Forces. I joined the U. S. Air Force, and from college to the military the party continued. I did well in the military continuing in the field of art as an illustrator. I continued my studies and was quickly promoted and became a Non-Commissioned Officer. Things were fine, I loved life.

After completing four years in the military, I received an honorable discharge, and the party was still on. Only this time there was an awareness I never had before. Something was not right. I found myself laughing on the outside and crying on the inside. Something seemed to be telling me that life was more than this party I was experiencing. There was a dead sick feeling on the inside. It was as if someone on the inside was crying out for help.

By this time in life I had married and fathered two children, however, that did not relieve the misery or the emptiness I was feeling inside. Well, thank God in 1971, by faith I received Jesus Christ as my Savior, and that emptiness was filled. I wish I could tell you that from that day until now I experienced total victory, however, that would be a lie. The truth is, that for seven years following my salvation conversion I was miserable. Yes! that's right, I was miserable after salvation. That's the reason God had me pen this handbook. Many of my brothers and sisters in the Lord are facing the same kind of misery I faced.

1

Forword (cont.)

I am certain that much of the misery I experienced was the result of spiritual ignorance. In other words a lack of knowledge. At that time I did not know how I was to live out the abundant life in Christ.

Now I know, and God would have me share this knowledge with others. As One of God's called pastors and teachers I want all believers to have this vital information, and live the victorious life God desires us to have. For seven years I experienced defeat as a Christian, from 1971-1978. Thank God, He showed me my down fall. In 1978 I was broken to be fixed. When nothing seemed to be working for me as a Christian I cried out to the Lord. "Lord , why is it nothing seems to work for me?" "I am saved!" It was at that place, God gave me this revelation. He said, "yes Wayne you are saved because you accepted me as your SAVIOR, but you would not allow me to be your LORD." A light came on! I could plainly see what God was saying. I knew I was a sinner, and I wanted Him to save me from a burning hell, but I still wanted things my way. I had not allowed Him to be my LORD. I was saved, I was apart of God's awesome army, but because of my ignorance I was a poor soldier. If you are saved you are in God's army. I pray this book will enlighten you to the point of wanting to be a GOOD SOLDIER.

G. Wayne Parker

A WORD OF KNOWLEDGE

"If you agree with what God has planned for your life on earth, you will discover your success."

Welcome to Boot Camp !

First of all, I want to sincerely congratulate you in your choice in becoming a member of God's family. However, it is vitally important to understand that you have also joined God's army. It is God's desire that all Christians be made aware of our place as soldiers in this world. If the family of God is to be successful here on earth we must learn to take a spiritual, militant type posture against the enemy.

In order for the Body of Christ to be effective in the earth we must be knowledgeable and mature in the Word of God. Read (Romans 12:1-2). Notice the word serves. The Church is God's armed force here on earth. Men and women are in service, on active duty for the Almighty God. Historically, the Church has not been thought of as an army of servicemen on active duty in this world. This has been one of our short comings. The Church is an awesome fighting unit that is on call by God twenty-four seven.

This study tool has been written to assist believers in renewing their minds. THINK ARMY! The Body of Christ is God's army. THINK SOLDIER! Every true believer is one of God's soldiers. THINK WAR! As Christians we are in spiritual warfare on earth. We must understand the fact that we are an awesome fighting force. One unit in Him, fighting the good fight of faith. Read (St. John 17:11, and 1 Timothy 6:12). Again, Welcome! May God Bless you soldier, and remember God's promise to us. We win!

The Church is God's armed force here on earth!

Fight the good fight of faith, lay hold on eternal life, where unto thou art called, and hast professed a good profession before many witnesses. 1 Timothy 6:12

GOD'S ARMY

CHAPTER I
Recruitment

A WORD OF KNOWLEDGE

"God wants you to be successful, He is drawing you to a place of success in Him."

Recruitment... God has always wanted you!

Recruitment is the act of recruiting or bringing one into a body such as an army. The purpose of recruiting is to supply an army with new personnel. A recruiter is one who brings in new army personnel called recruits or enlisted men.

Jesus says no man can come to him except the Father which sent him draws them (St. John 6:44). This means God Himself is the recruiter of His own army. It is obvious by the Word of God that from the beginning of creation, God had a thought out plan, not only to be man's creator, but to be man's God, man's Lord and man's friend. God has always wanted you!

In the beginning, we find God giving man all he needed (Genesis 1:27-31). It was because of man's disobedience that all humanity became enemies of God. Yet, God has been reaching out to draw man back to himself. Satan, the original enemy of God is the one that led mankind to the fall (Genesis chapter 3). When man sinned against God we all fell captive to Satan. However, since that horrible ordeal, God has graciously given everyone an opportunity to escape the enemy's horrible prison death camp.

Yes! God recruits all those who are willing to join!

Recruitment..... God has always wanted you!

Come unto me all who labour and are heavy laden and I will give you rest (Matthew 11:28). This is a call to life in Christ, which is eternal life in God. This call goes to all mankind, each and every one. The call of God's recruitment has no racial, cultural, or moral prejudices. God says that whomever chooses to come, can come by way of their God given faith and free will. All that choose to come, can come (St. Mark 8:34).

Jesus says all that the father gives him, will come to him and those that come to him he will not cast them out (St. John 6:37). When God says come join me, He is actually recruiting us. He's pointing His finger of love at all of us and saying, "I Want You!" First, He wants us in His family, and at the same time, He's recruiting us into His mighty army. What an awesome privilege. If you have received Jesus Christ as your savior, you are no longer considered his enemy. You have answered the call. You are now on the Lord's side. Your destiny has been settled. You have eternal placement in God (St. John 3:15-16). No child of God needs to be afraid of death in the physical, because our spirits have eternal life, meaning, (life without breech, break or any interval).

Thank God, we have been recruited into a life and mission with God. God has always wanted you!

GOD'S ARMY

CHAPTER II
Enlistment

A WORD OF KNOWLEDGE

"Don't let your past block your successful future in Christ."

Enlistment....................Joining God's Army

When we by means of free will have accepted the Lord Jesus Christ as our personal Savior, we at that moment became members of His mighty army. God now addresses us as soldiers. When we gave our life to Christ, we enlisted. Yes, we have joined God's Army. There are a host of scriptures God has given us to renew our minds to think in more of a militant fashion. (see Biblical Glossary) As you read the scripture given below it will be obvious that God has called the Church to be His visible armed force here on earth.

In the second chapter of Philippians, Paul as he writes to the church mentions one of his companions in the faith. Notice the various titles he gives to this fellow believer called Epaphroditus. _My brother,_ and _companion in labour_, and _fellowsoldier_ (Phillipians 2:25). FELLOW SOLDIER ! Did you get that? As brothers and sisters in the Lord we are also enlisted fellow soldiers in the army of the Lord. What a privilege!

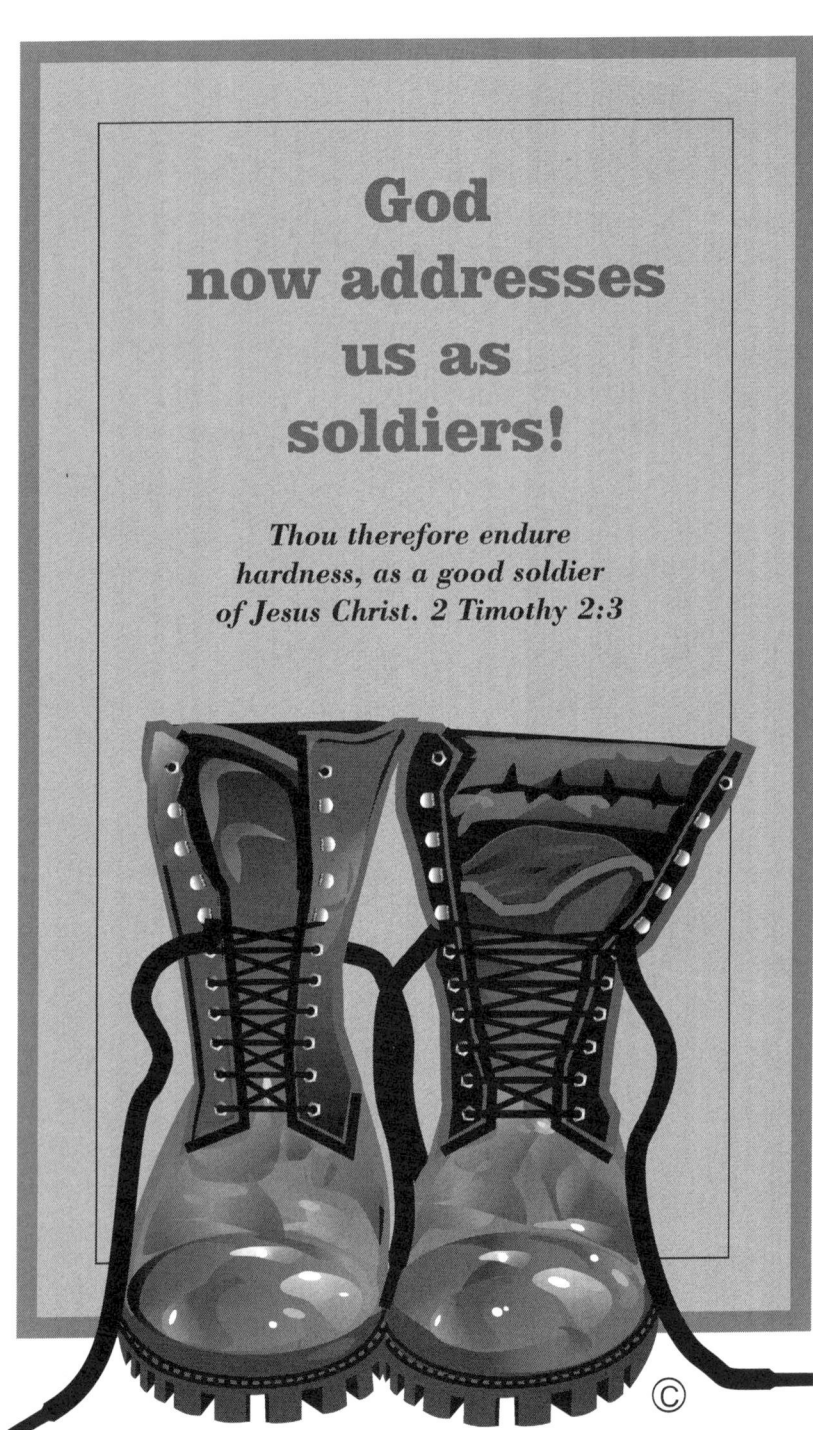

God now addresses us as soldiers!

Thou therefore endure hardness, as a good soldier of Jesus Christ. 2 Timothy 2:3

GOD'S ARMY

CHAPTER III
The
Bus
Ride...in

A WORD OF KNOWLEDGE

"During times of future turbulence, it will be the Word of God that stabilizes you, not your emotions."

The BUS RIDE.................in

It was a cool brisk Thursday morning in the month of March. The Greyhound bus was swiftly roaring down the blacktop highway. The sun was beginning to peer over the distant hills as Ethan Christian gazed from the smeared window four seats from the entry of the bus. It had been a long restless night, and Ethan had gotten very little sleep in anticipation of his arrival at the military training camp. The new recruit had just recently decided to join the armed forces, and he was very excited about his newly found adventure.

As the bus continued its steady trek down the three lane highway, the glaring sun slowly revealed more of its awesome brightness. Ethan reached into his left inside pocket pulling out a pair of green tinted sun glasses. He slowly placed the shades over his eyes in an attempt to make himself a bit more comfortable. Slouching down in his seat he pulled the collar of his lightweight brown jacket up around his neck, hoping to get a little more sleep before his arrival at the camp's induction center. Ethan closed his weary eyes and slowly sank further into his seat.

Just as he began to drift into a deep sleep the fifty passenger Greyhound bus suddenly jerked and swerved off the highway rumbling over the gravel shoulder of the road. Ethan was rudely awakened by a horrible screeching sound. A soda bottle rolled down the aisle slamming against the adjacent seat.

The bus had run over a large remnant of metal cargo, and it had lodged itself under the front bumper of the bus. The swerve of the huge bus had thrown Ethan to the far side of his seat. He was obviously shaken from the awkward movements of the bus.

Ethan's heart was pounding against his chest, and after a deep gasp he slowly pulled himself up to see what the commotion was all about. Thank God! Everything was under control. The bus driver had brilliantly steered the bus back onto the highway, Ethan sighed in relief.

After all the commotion Ethan's mind began to recall past events that had threatened his life. His mind rolled backwards as if it were a CD on rewind. His mind replayed several death threatening moments. One after another past dangers resurfaced flashing before him with alarming clarity. During that brief episode one thing stood out with bright intensity, it had been the grace of God that had allowed him to still be alive. It could have only been God that had allowed him to escape death from birth to this point in his life. It had been God for sure.

Now that the sudden fear had subsided Ethan decided to continue his nap. Again he closed his eyes and drifted off to sleep. Soon the bus had reached the terminal where someone would be waiting for him. This time it was the voice of the bus driver that woke him from his peaceful sleep on the way in.

Waiting at the bus terminal was a short stern looking Military Sergeant. He quickly boarded the bus loudly encouraging all recruits to follow his lead. Ethan then trailed the sergeant towards the bus depot where other recruits stood waiting for direction. Inside was another sergeant, well dressed holding a sign that read, "ALL ARMY RECRUITS LINE UP HERE." Ethan hurriedly ran over to the corner where the sergeant stood. Excited and curious about his future, he kept his eyes focused on the sergeant. He sat his torn battered suitcase on the floor near the light gray wall. The well dressed sergeant began calling out names in alphabetical order: Adams, Brock, Chapman, and so on. Finally the sergeant shouted Christian, and Ethan stepped forward with the others.

After every recruits' name had been called they were ordered to follow their guide to a small army green bus waiting outside. All the recruits seemed to mount with excitement. At the same time they were in deep thought anticipating their basic training. What would it be like? How long was the ride to the base? The small bus pulled away from the greyhound terminal and the excitement heighten as they got closer, and closer to the military base camp.

Finally the bus came to a gate with a guard on post, waving them through as they continued their BUS RIDE IN. When the bus stopped near a tan painted building the door opened, and a Master Sergeant boarded the bus. "WELCOME!" He said with a loud boisterous voice. "Get off the bus!"

The Rude Awakening!

Immediately after getting off, the sergeant says, "We are counting on you to go back out there and be great champions. Go out there and be all you can be." Ethan and his fellow recruits found themselves walking away with nothing but their old battered luggage, and a word of encouragement. Just imagine that. After that long, and exciting BUS RIDE IN.

Every week, however, they were to return to the base camp to celebrate their victorious new life. Can you believe that? What kind of army would actually send new recruits out on a battle field without any training? Sad to say but this has been the initial plight of a host of born again Christians. They join the local church never receiving the knowledge or training they need for Christian Warfare. When they began their life in Christ, the enemy was waiting right outside the gate. In some cases he shot at them before ever leaving the base camp. Right there in the church, they were attacked by the enemy. Perhaps it was a enemy spy, or an immature Christian used by Satan in an act of rudeness, speaking negatively towards others. Soldiers actually wounded from the very beginning. You will learn more about spies at the end of chapter 7.

Yes, getting off the proverbial bus of Christian conversion can really be a RUDE AWAKENING.

GOD'S ARMY

CHAPTER IV

Analogy of

The
Bus
Ride...in

A WORD OF KNOWLEDGE

"God did not save us to take us on a guilt trip, He saved us to help us stop tripping."

Analogy of the Bus Ride

Ethan Christian's rude awakening would never be the case with someone joining the Armed Forces of America. If such a thing were to happen to one of our sons or daughters enlisting in the military we would be outraged. We would have great concern for their lives in a state of war. We would have concern because they were never properly trained or equipped for war.

Sadly, Ethan Christian's bus ride typifies the path multitudes of Christians have experienced upon entry into the body of Christ (God's Armed Forces). When a person accepts Jesus Christ as their savior, joy fills their heart (spirit). However, if they are not trained, and made aware of the spiritual warfare they are facing, they will experience much instability. Many have been left to walk through life's new gateway stumbling, falling, and scrambling on their own.

Christianity is more than a ticket to heaven, or the gift of eternal life. Christians are called to occupy the earth as God's soldiers. We have been given a clear assigned purpose as God's army. Like Ethan and his torn battered luggage, many Christians sat their torn battered lives down at the church door only to be ordered to go back out there and live the victorious Christian life. Many are living defeated lives simply because they have never been trained for the inevitable spiritual warfare we all now face.

Christians are called to occupy the earth as God's soldiers!

And he called his ten servants, and delivered them ten pounds, and said unto them Occupy till I come. Luke 19:13

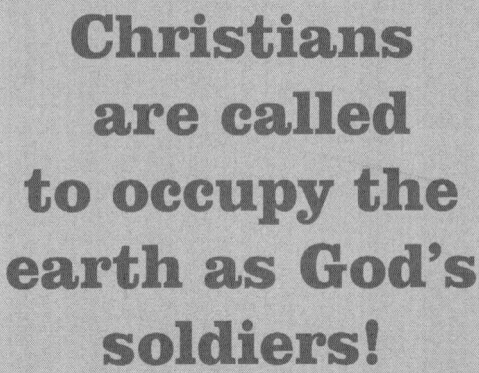

GOD'S ARMY

CHAPTER V
Battle

A WORD OF KNOWLEDGE

"When your old mind wants to move in fear, compare the size of your problem to the size of your God."

"By faith trust what God allows."

Battle

As Christians we have been called to a life of spiritual battle. Ethan at least understood he was joining a unit of fighters. Sadly, most people enter Christianity with a mind that only seeks refuge. Certainly all of us need spiritual refuge, and thank God we do have an awesome place of refuge in Jesus Christ. We are spiritually positioned in God (Col 3:3). We are going to heaven, and we are being kept by the power of God. But why are we left down here? Why did God not whisk us off to heaven? Instead, He left us here for a given space of time. Why is that?

We are here to fight (Battle) against the forces of evil. We are here to war against the powers of darkness. It's a spiritual battle. *For the weapons of our warfare are not carnal but mighty through God to the pulling down of strong holds,* (2 Corinthians 10:4). This scripture clearly expresses our purpose in war. We are to fight in an all out effort to loose the hold of the enemy over those who are held captive. Jesus came to set the captives free, and that work is to continue as He uses His Church by the power of the Holy Spirit. We have been called to battle. Fight the good fight of faith (1Timothy 6:12).

Like Ethan, many Christians were waiting with great anticipation, and excitement, looking to be led into a victorious life, only to be told, get off the bus and get to work in the church. Get busy for the Lord. So they hurried their way onto choirs, usher boards, and other church ministries.

Some were even placed in leadership position knowing nothing about the battle or spiritual warfare. This neglect has produced a host of confused, and defeated Christians. They are set back by their lack of knowledge. This is the scenario of far too many of our brothers and sisters, fellow soldiers, recruits, and enlisted personnel. Too many are wondering around on the battlefields of Christian life wounded, and devastated. Some have been forcefully preached to, preached at, others were put to work, but never having been trained in spiritual warfare. Jesus said, "take my yoke upon you and learn of me." (St. Matthew 11:29) Jesus came with power to battle the enemy, and after He ascended into heaven He gave power to the Church (Ephesians 6:10). Power to do what? Power to fight His enemies. If you are a true Christian you have been given the power to fight, or, to battle. However, we must all be trained for war. We must obtain knowledge, wisdom, and spiritual strategies in order to stand against the enemy. Does that make sense to you? I truly hope so. Jesus wants us to have a victorious life here on earth. Yet, this will not happen without a fight, a good fight of faith (1Timothy 6:12). Fight! Fight! Fight!

It is our prayer that the Body of Christ will mature, unify, and be the power force we are called to be. This will take both individual and collective commitment. Training and more training in the Word of God. BOOT CAMP for Christian soldiers.

Now that you see we are called to battle, here's good news, this handbook was especially written to provide the basic training knowledge we all need to be victorious as soldiers. This handbook has been created via God's Word. It is to help you think and act like a good soldier of Jesus Christ (2 Timothy 2:3). Again, welcome to BOOT CAMP for Christians. You're in God's Army now.

Battle
Operation
Occupancy
Training
Camp... FOR CHRISTIANS

This is how it should have been for Ethan after the proverbial bus ride in. As soon as he entered boot camp, an instructor should have been right there to teach him.

Soldier! This is who you are!

    This is your uniform!

    This is your weapon!

Upon entry into the armed forces a recruit is issued a study manual, a uniform, a weapon, and training starts immediately. We must operate under authority, discipline, and orders sent from our Commander, and Chief, Jesus Christ. As Christians we must know how we are to operate in the earth, and in order for us to operate as a unit we must clearly understand who we are as Christians, our uniform and our God given weaponry. As soldiers we are to be equipped for battle (spiritual warfare).

We have been called to battle!

For the weapons of our warfare are not carnal, but mighty through God to the pulling down of strong holds;
2 Corinthians 10:4

GOD'S ARMY

CHAPTER VI
Operations

A WORD OF KNOWLEDGE

"The only way your way works, is when your way becomes His way."

"If you want to be a successful, victorious soldier you must love God's Word more then the <u>old you</u> loves other things."

Operation

"Soldier... who are you?" Now that you have accepted the call to be a soldier; what are the benefits? How are we positioned, and seen in the eyes of God? When joining a fighting unit a soldier needs to feel secure. The recruit needs to be assured he or she has a trustworthy support system. Philippians 4:19 expresses God supplying all of our needs, that would include, (food, clothing, shelter, etc.), God knows what we need.

Every military unit wants its soldiers to believe they will be victorious at the end of the war. God's Word promises the Church that very thing. We are more than conquerors (Rom. 8:37). Not only are we told we are winners, we have already won in Christ. As a vital part of our military spiritual training we must know who we are, and how we are positioned here on earth. We must know our position as believers.

When we accepted Jesus Christ as Savior we joined a body of believers called the Church, His Body. At that moment we were placed, and sanctioned as His.

CHOSEN: We are chosen in God, who knows all things. He knew before the foundation of the world those who would one day say yes to His call by way of the death and resurrection of His Son Jesus Christ. Having already accepted us in His foreknowledge we are chosen people of God, read (2 Thessalonians 2:13) for additional enlightenment.

SEALED: We are a sealed people, meaning we have been marked, or stamped as God's property, we are His, read (Ephesians 1:13; 4:30). This is a wonderful truth that should give us all awesome mental stability. This is our positional sanctification, guaranteed by the Spirit.

KEPT: We are not kept by our Christian behavior, although we are certainly called to behave ourselves. As soldiers of God we are to follow His commands, but, we are kept in spiritual placement in Christ by God Himself. Read (1 Peter 1:5) to find this truth. This is the positional security we have in Christ.

CHILDREN OF LIGHT: We are no longer in a place of spiritual darkness. We are now in the light of God's love, read (1 Thessalonians 5:5). As God's soldiers we are to be guides for those desiring to come out of darkness. We are the lights of the world, and we must be on post. You are one of God's lights on post here on earth. This is the practical sanctification we should live out.

HOLY: Although we are still pulled by, or influenced by the world, the flesh (old mind) and the devil, our enemies. We have been positioned or spiritually placed in God. We are sanctioned as righteous and holy. Although your emotions may not always agree with this, it's who God says you are, and you are to operate as such. We are a righteous, and holy people. Read the following scriptures, (2 Corinthians 5:21; Ephesians 1:4).

SAVED: We have been saved from a terrible eternal separation from God, and His goodness. The Bible points out a horrible existence of separation, called hell. Hell is an eternal separation from the almighty, true and living God.

God is absolutely good. The absence of any portion of good could only offer an absolute state of evil. By accepting the sacrifice of Jesus Christ God's Son we receive eternal life with Him. This means we have a life that will never end (life without breech, break, or any interval). To reject Jesus Christ would mean one chooses an eternal existence, separated from God, and surrounded by absolute evil. Hell is a burning torment of the spirit. All true Christians have been eternally saved from such a horrible existence. Thank God! Read (1 Timothy 2:3-6; Ephesians 2:5-9; Acts 15:11). Soldiers, even when we physically dissolve, our spirits go to a better state of life. What a wonderful salvation!

BORN AGAIN: Being born again actually means our dead spirits (dead in that we were detached from God who is life) become alive by being reunited with God. We are born again, now, not in a physical newness, but in a spiritual newness. We are actually born from above. We are changed and made alive by the Spirit of God through faith in Jesus Christ. Read (Romans 10:9-10). Just think of this. God is in us and we are in Him eternally. If you are a Christian you are a born again soldier.

SANCTIFIED: This classification is actually the same as being made Holy. We have been positioned in Christ. Set apart for His use. We have been purified in the spirit, and consecrated for God's kingdom work. Read (Hebrews 10:10; 1 Corinthians 6:11) to see just how special we are as God's Special Army of soldiers.

We started this chapter on operation by addressing Christians as soldiers. That should be our thinking. We are God's soldiers! But how should a good soldier operate in the military? If there is one thing that will wreck the life of a soldier it's disobedience. When a soldier is seriously out of order he is isolated, thrown in the brig, cut off from normal fellowship with other soldiers. If he or she refuses to submit to set authority they will find themselves in a miserable state of being. So it is with God's Army, God is a stickler for order. When Satan moved out of order in heaven he was kicked out. God will not stand for disorder or confusion in His Church, the Body of Christ. So it is of vital importance that each soldier steps or marches in an orderly manner. All of the works of the Church should be done in decency, and in order. Although true Christians have eternal life, our lives on earth can be made miserable if we insist on moving in rebellion and disobedience. As good soldiers we are called to obey His commands.

All of us have an obligation to line up with the order God has established in the Church. If an army is to be successful there must be set order. Each soldier must submit to a code of conduct. As soldiers in God's Army, our code of conduct is to walk in obedience to God's Word. We are to study the Bible, and obey God's instructions using the life of Christ as our example. To follow our Lord Jesus Christ is the walk of a good soldier. We are to operate based on who we are by the leading of the Holy Spirit. He is our lead officer.

We are to live a life becoming of servicemen (Romans 12:1). We all have been called to live a disciplined life, a life pleasing to our Lord, and Savior, Jesus Christ. Many Christians struggle to operate in righteousness. They become confused because although they are saved, (born again) they are not living out the life of victory, meaning they don't have the joy and peace God desires them to have. How could such a thing occur in the life of a believer? At this point we need to address the matter of Lordship, something that is rarely taught.

Lordship is a state of Christian maturity in which one surrenders all: spirit, soul (mind), and body. There are many Christians who have been living lives of defeat because they chose to move according to self-will after salvation. They are saved because of the spirit work of the cross, however, they are living defeated lives because they are either untaught and ignorant of the Word, or they are simply wilfully disobedient. They have received Jesus Christ as Savior, but not as Lord over their lives here on earth. If we are to be successful as God's soldiers in this life, we must surrender totally to God's will for our lives. A good soldier must adhere to the voice of the Commander and Chief. Jesus asked this question, "Why call me Lord, Lord and do not what I say?" Today He is still asking Christians the same question. Check (Luke 6:46). It is of utmost importance that we relinquish our will to God after salvation. Let His will be done in you.

As Christians we must understand our tripartite make-up. We are Spirit, Soul, and Body. The spirit portion of our being is what has been reborn, and made new. Read (2 Corinthians 5:17). The spirit of man is the real person, the true man after the likeness of God. God is a Spirit and they that worship Him must worship Him in spirit and in truth (St. John 4:24). We read scriptures declaring our spirits sealed and made righteous, yet we must not forget we have two other parts of our being. These are our soul, the mental emotional realm, and our bodies (1 Thessalonians 5:23). Our spirit was made new, however, our mind and body were not. God therefore instructs us to renew our minds with His Word, and this is the only way one could possibly present their body a living sacrifice Holy and acceptable unto God. (Romans 12:1-2).

God has already changed our spirits, now he calls us to change our minds. As our minds change in accord with God's Word, the body is transformed in its deeds. We begin to walk in a manner of life that pleases God. Look at what (Galations 5:16) has to say.

As God's Army on earth, we are to operate in obedience to His commands. We have been given an awesome spiritual position for operating on earth. We now trust that you understand who you are. You are CHOSEN, SEALED, CHILDREN OF LIGHT. You are HOLY, SAVED, BORN AGAIN, SANCTIFIED, and a SOLDIER. That's you!

GOD'S ARMY

CHAPTER VII
Occupancy

A WORD OF KNOWLEDGE

"As a Christian soldier, you are called to stand. You cannot stand right when you are standing for wrong."

Occupancy

Have you ever asked yourself these questions: Why am I here? Why are we here ? The Church; What is our purpose here on earth? It would seem that after Jesus Christ paid our sin price on the cross he could have simply taken all believers to heaven, yet He left us down here. Why did He do that?

After the resurrection of Jesus Christ, He declared all power had been given unto Him in heaven and in earth (Matthew 28:18). He then ascended into heaven. Why did He not take all believers with Him at that point? Well, the answer is He had a work for us to do. The Church, the Body of Christ was left to occupy the earth. We are to assist Him in His plan of redemption. That is, we are to operate as soldiers, not in heaven, but right here on earth! Read this scripture (St. Luke 19:13), here Jesus is sharing the parable of stewardship or service. Service...Service!

Christians are given gifts, and talents , and we are expected to make use of them by making a spiritual investment on earth. The word occupy is a military term. It does not mean simply take up space. When an army is told to occupy, they are to hold in check a given territory or position. After Jesus stripped Satan of the power he had over us he then gave power to the Church to keep the enemy under. Ephesians 1:19-23, tells us that Christ has transferred power to the Church. One day our Savior will return for us (Acts 1:11).

When Jesus Christ returns as King of the earth, He will subdue His enemies, and take full control in the earth. In the mean time the Church has been given the power, and the authority to fight against the powers of darkness. Read (Luke 10:19). We have a job. We must accomplish the work assigned to us.

In Matthew 11:29, Jesus says " take my yoke upon you and learn of me." In other words we are to study the works and ways of our Lord. This is apart of our training. 2 Timothy 2:15 tells us to study to show ourselves approved. This means we should be diligent, prompt, endeavoring in labor, and study. There should be structured study preparing us for spiritual warfare. We train, we fight, and we stand against the enemy. Yes! We are called to remain, and occupy until He comes. Read this scripture for confirmation (Luke 19:13).

As we occupy the earth we must make sure we know the Word of God concerning the strategies of the enemy. Just as there are spies in natural warfare, there are also spies in spiritual warfare. The Bible speaks of those that crept in unaware. These are spies in the church camp. People who pretend they are saved, however they are there to do the work of the enemy (Jude 1:4). As good soldiers we should be able to detect or discern lights because Satan can appear as an angel of light (2 Corinthians 11:14).

GOD'S ARMY

CHAPTER VIII
Training

A WORD OF KNOWLEDGE

"You must allow the truth of God's Word to surpass the content of your human intellect to have peace of mind."

'If you trust the stability of God's Word you can trust the movement of His hand."

Training

No army that is serious about warfare would send a soldier off to battle without proper training. In a regular army much of the training would consist of much rigorous physical training. However, because the Christian warfare is spiritual, our focus must be mainly that of a spiritual nature. The training we need is more spiritual and mental than physical. For the weapons of our warfare are not carnal, (physical) but mighty through God to the pulling down of strong holds; (2 Corinthians 10:4).

I must stress this point. Spiritual power is much greater than the powers of mind and body. Spiritual power is the foundation for both mental and physical powers. In (Romans 12:2) we are told our transformation in this world is to be processed by way of a renewed mind. Our movements are from spirit, to mind, to body. This is the method in which our physical is to be presented acceptable unto God. This is our reasonable service.

This truth is extremely important because the main battle after salvation is in the mind. The enemy can attack both the physical and the mental, these attacks are efforts to get us to retreat in our faith, (the power of the spirit). In Matthew 4:4, Jesus told Satan (who is our enemy) that man shall not live by bread alone but by every Word that proceeds out of the mouth of God. The Holy Bible is God's Word and His Word is our manual for training. Read (Hosea 4:6).

In that scripture it tells us that the people of God perish for lack of knowledge. As Christian soldiers we must be students of God's Word. Knowing God's Word actually sets a perimeter of defense against false prophets. When we know the Word of God a wall of protection is being formed around our minds. As soldiers in a ready position for spiritual battle we are to gird up the lions of our mind (1 Peter 1:13). This means every Christian is to be wrapped tight. Mentally sound and standing ready against the attacks directed towards our minds. 2 Timothy 1:7 says God has not given us a spirit of fear but of power and love and a sound mind. That's for you !

At this juncture we need to be sure you understand the human make-up or composition we have previously mentioned. We are tripartite beings. That simply means we are created with three parts. These three parts are <u>Spirit</u>, <u>Soul</u>, and <u>Body</u>. All of these parts are also made up of three parts, See Diagram A. Remember this, we are a spirit, we have a soul (mind), and we live in a body. The spirit and soul are the invisible areas and the body is the visible portion. Our spirit portion is the foundation, or base of our tripartite being. Knowing this is vital. As we mentioned before, the spirit has been sealed by God. The enemy cannot touch this portion of our being after we are in Christ. Read (1 Peter 1:3-5; 23). We must learn how to protect ourselves from attacks in the mind, and body; especially attacks in the mind. It is the main battle ground. We must equip our minds.

Man..........................(Tripartite) (1 THESSALONIANS 5:23)

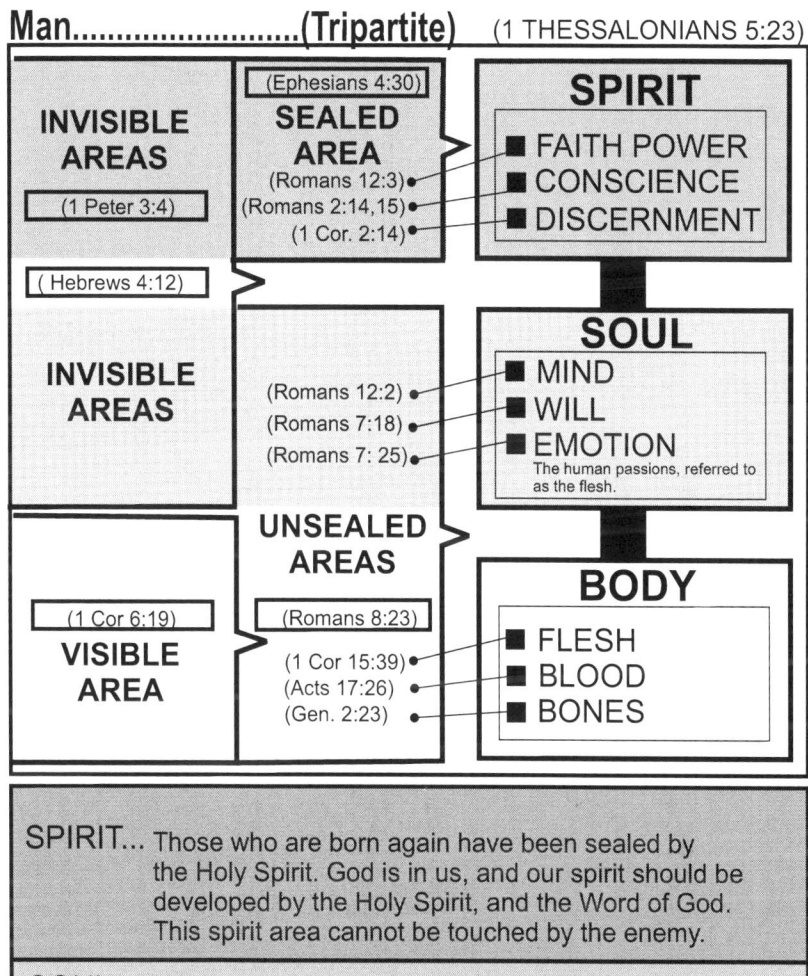

INVISIBLE AREAS (1 Peter 3:4)	(Ephesians 4:30) **SEALED AREA** (Romans 12:3) (Romans 2:14,15) (1 Cor. 2:14)	**SPIRIT** ■ FAITH POWER ■ CONSCIENCE ■ DISCERNMENT
(Hebrews 4:12)		
INVISIBLE AREAS	(Romans 12:2) (Romans 7:18) (Romans 7:25)	**SOUL** ■ MIND ■ WILL ■ EMOTION The human passions, referred to as the flesh.
	UNSEALED AREAS	
(1 Cor 6:19) **VISIBLE AREA**	(Romans 8:23) (1 Cor 15:39) (Acts 17:26) (Gen. 2:23)	**BODY** ■ FLESH ■ BLOOD ■ BONES

SPIRIT... Those who are born again have been sealed by the Holy Spirit. God is in us, and our spirit should be developed by the Holy Spirit, and the Word of God. This spirit area cannot be touched by the enemy.

SOUL... Our soul is not sealed by the Holy Spirit, and is always subject to attacks from the enemy. This is the main battle ground of spiritual warfare. This is the area that needs to be renewed in It's thinking based on God's Word; (Mind / Will / Emotions).

BODY... The process of victory moves from the Holy Spirit, to our spirit, to the soul (mind, will, emotions), and then to the body. Our bodies are to be used as visible tools of God. The deeds done in our bodies should glorify God.

© G. Wayne Parker   Diagram A

Now that we know we are in a war we must realize our enemies. Notice I said enemies not enemy. If you were to ask the average Christian who our enemy is, most would say the Devil, or Satan. This answer would be correct, however, we as Christians are not only at war with Satan. We war against his entire system (Ephesians 6:12). This system of darkness includes demons (fallen angels). Within that system we also find two others enemies known as the world, and the flesh, (carnal/worldly thinking and actions)

When a soldier receives training for warfare a vital part of that training is to be able to identify the enemy. If soldiers are not equipped to recognized the enemy he or she will fire on their own. They will wound fellow soldiers. This is a tragedy an army could certainly do without. An army should never fight against its own. If we are fighting each other, the enemy can simply stand back, and laugh with hearty vigor. The Army of God must be one that is unified and can detect the movements of the enemy within, or without.

When Satan chose to go against God he then became God's enemy. Satan now controls the realm of darkness which works against God, His Word and His people. God allowed Satan to test or entice mankind (Adam and Eve) and the outcome was devastating. Mankind fell away from a spiritual union with God. This is known as the fall of man. Because of sin (disobedience), mankind was separated from God. This removal was a spiritual death that fell on us all.

Humanity fell into darkness under satanic control. Because of the fall of man, Satan was then able to gain a dominate position over all humanity. Satan gained rule over the human mind. Mankind from that point was programmed to operate in darkness, and to walk in a lifestyle that is centered around sin, and to continued evil.

This is what the Bible declares as the FLESH. When the Bible speaks of the flesh as God's enemy it is talking about minds and bodies that now operate under a system headed by Satan himself. This state of being is also known as carnality or carnal mindedness. Minds and bodies driven by ungodly appetites, and pleasures (Romans 8:5-8). At this point let me make this clear. God is not against our physical bodies, He simply wants them operating in righteousness according to His Word (1Corinthians 6:13; Romans 12:1,2). Because of sin mankind was separated from God. Man's mind was set to operate as a enemy to God. This is the flesh, the old mind, the old nature, the old man.

The third enemy is called the WORLD. This is simply the satanic system of darkness which ignores, and refuses to adapt to the Word of God. This system holds its own rules, and ways. It's a system constantly luring mankind in the wrong direction. This system of darkness cares nothing about what God says is right or wrong (1 Corinthians 1:20-25). The Word of God proclaims anyone that is a friend with the world to be a enemy of God (James 4:4). Three enemies: the DEVIL, the FLESH, and the WORLD.

Although this satanic system works against God, He does not want to destroy the people held captive in the system (John 3:16). Jesus Christ did not come to wipe out humanity. He came to free those trapped in that system. Jesus came to set us free. God is not angry with fallen humanity, He pities us. Look at what God says to us in (John 3: 17) about Him.

So again these are our three main enemies, the DEVIL (Satan), the FLESH, and the WORLD. We must contend with all three. However, the enemy that gives us the most trouble individually is not the devil himself, but the FLESH. The reason this is true is because the flesh, or the old mind lingers with us. Every day this old man fights against our new spirit, and renewed mind. It still wants to control our bodies. It still wants to disregard God's Word, and use our bodies. This is why it is vital that our minds be renewed, and guarded (Romans 12:2; 1 Peter 1:13). As born again soldiers of God we should be reprogrammed, and operating under our new system of life. A system which is programmed by the Word of God. The Bible is our training manual. Two of our enemies work from the outside, tempting, and luring us. The flesh, however, is working from the inside like a spy. No matter where we go the spy is there, but no matter where the attacks are coming from I have good news! God has given us the power to defeat all three enemies (1Corinthians 9:27; Romans 6:14). Yes, by God's power we can do this.

We are God's Army, His soldiers! Yes, we have enemies, three of them. It may on the surface appear unfair, but remember this! The Almighty God is on our side. If God be for us who can be against us. At the end of the war we win. We are already winners in Jesus Christ, our Savior, our Lord, our Champion. Greater is He that is in us than he that is in the world. Read all of the following scriptures (Luke 10:19; 1 John 4:4; Romans 8:37). We are called to fight, and fight good. We can do this soldier! Fight Good (1 Timothy 6:12)! By faith we are to trust God in spiritual warfare. We should trust Him to be all we need Him to be. If God be for us who can win against us? We can fight this war resting in the promises of God. God has not given us the spirit of fear; but of power, and of love and of a sound mind (2 Timothy 1:7). From the book of Genesis to the book of Revelation God's people have been given the command to fear not. Trust God Soldier!

As Christian Soldiers we must be students of God's Word!

Study to shew thyself approved unto God, a workman that needeth not be ashamed, rightly dividing the word of truth. 2 Timothy 2:15

GOD'S ARMY

CHAPTER IX

Code of Conduct

A WORD OF KNOWLEDGE

"If you humble yourself before God you will have no place to go but up."

Code Of Conduct

When recruits are inducted into the regular army they are at that time expected to live disciplined quality lives. They are trained for warfare, however, soldiers are expected to carry themselves in an honorable manner at all times. In 2 Timothy 2:3,4 Paul says, as good soldiers of Jesus Christ we are to endure hardness, and that no soldier will entangle himself with the ways of the world if he wants to please God. In other words it is vitally important that every Christian demonstrates godly behavior. Soldiers in a regular army are given what is called A CODE OF CONDUCT. It's the same in God's Army. We receive commandments from our Commander and Chief Jesus Christ regarding our behavior here on earth. Matthew 7:20 tells us that by their fruits we will know them. Christian soldiers should be identified not only by their uniformed appearance, but by their righteous conduct. The Bible reveals this conduct as the fruit of the spirit (Galatians 5:22,23). Our Christian character should exhibit love, joy, peace, longsuffering (patience), gentleness, goodness, faith, meekness, and temperance (self control). This should be our Christlike Conduct.

To be a good soldier our conduct must correspond with our profession. If we say we are Christians, then we should demonstrate this in our day to day conduct. A good soldier should not operate in conduct unbecoming a Christian. Many Christians seem to think that being skillful in their gifts and talents will please God regardless of their conduct. This is wrong.

The Word of God declares misconduct as sin. It is not pleasing to God when Christians are out of order. It was because of misconduct that God had Paul address the unruly Church in Corinth. There were dissensions, and other ungodly conduct operating in the Church. Paul had to write to them giving them correction, and guidance. Their conduct was not becoming that of Christians. Thank God for all His drill instructors.

Soldiers in a regular army who prove to be undisciplined on or off duty are reprimanded, and some times released from duty with a dishonorable discharge. In the case of Christian soldiers who move out of order, the Lord will chasten (discipline) and scourge (harsher discipline) Read (Hebrews 12:4-10). There may also be cases where sin or misbehavior will result in physical death. The Lord will at times remove the disobedient from their work on earth. Even though a true Christian has eternal life, their physical life could be shortened. A Christian whose life is taken because of disobedience is one who has been dishonorably removed from their earthly duty station. They are taken away because of unfruitfulness (1 John 5:16; Acts 5:9,10). As good soldiers we are to bear good fruit for the Master's use.

Yes, as good soldiers we are to live disciplined lives! Lives that exhibit a Christ likeness. Our lives should reflect the attributes of our Lord and Savior Jesus Christ. We are to study our training manual (The Holy Bible) and live according to His requirements for us as soldiers.

If we fall short of His requirement we are to run to Him, not from Him. When we sincerely repent of our sins He is faithful to forgive us. Soldiers who run from God will find themselves in deeper trouble (AWOL, Absent Without Leave). If you are out of order ask for forgiveness. God will help you do better by the power of the Holy Spirit. Just go to Him! The obedient life will usher us into the abundant life. Yes! Even in the heat of battle a good soldier can experience the peace, and joy of God (St John 10:10). In short, our **CODE OF CONDUCT** is to simply **WALK IN THE SPIRIT**. Do what you know is right as a Christian. If we walk in what we know is right we will avoid walking in what we know is wrong. Read Galatians chapter 5 and highlight verse 16.

Lives that exhibit a Christ likeness!

This I say then, walk in the Spirit, and ye shall not fulfill the lust of the flesh. Galatians 5:16

GOD'S ARMY

CHAPTER X
Uniform

A WORD OF KNOWLEDGE

"If your life as a Christian is in disguise, take off the old, and be distinguished."

"If you have truly changed the world should see the change."

Uniform

Here's your uniform soldier! When a new recruit joins the army a uniform is issued. The soldier is given apparel that matches his fellow soldiers. There is then a visual uniformity throughout the unit. When a Christian joins God's army he or she is clothed in the righteousness of God, and is to put on their new nature. Read this scripture, (Ephesians 4:24).

We are also given battle dress, or protective clothing. We are instructed to put it on (Ephesians 6:11), to be commanded to put on battle dress says it is your duty to dress right. It is not something automatic. We are to put on all of the battle armor of God, not a portion of it. All of it. Ephesians chapter 6:14-17 calls out each piece of battle dress or armor. See Diagram B, and study each piece. We must walk in the TRUTH of the Word of God. We must move as a RIGHTEOUS people, and as people of PEACE. Above all we must move by FAITH. We must walk with the assurance of SALVATION, and we must know the Word of God which is our SWORD OF THE SPIRIT. When we study each piece of our armour we find that each piece refers to our thinking, or our actions. If we think right, and walk up-right God says we are protected from the strategies of the enemy. With this battle dress uniform we can stand in warfare. When we are dressed right the enemy can shoot their best shot. We may receive a few dents or cracks in our armor, but darts of evil are unable to penetrate a fully armored soldier of God.

We should all be clothed alike with a distinct visible unity, and all marching to God's cadence. Rank and file in strategic order. The world should be impressed by our oneness in thinking, speaking, and actions. Read what it says in (Romans 15:6). When we are armored in Christ we then glorify God in our obedient likeness. We should all look like Jesus Christ, our Lord and Savior. Put on Christ, walk like Him, talk like Him. We are to put on faith, love, and salvation. We are to be dressed in light (1 Thessalonians 5:8; Romans 13:12). "Dress right, dress, soldier," put it on! Put on the Whole uniform of protection, and stand soldier.

Be Uniform, and In-Line
"Dress Right, Dress"

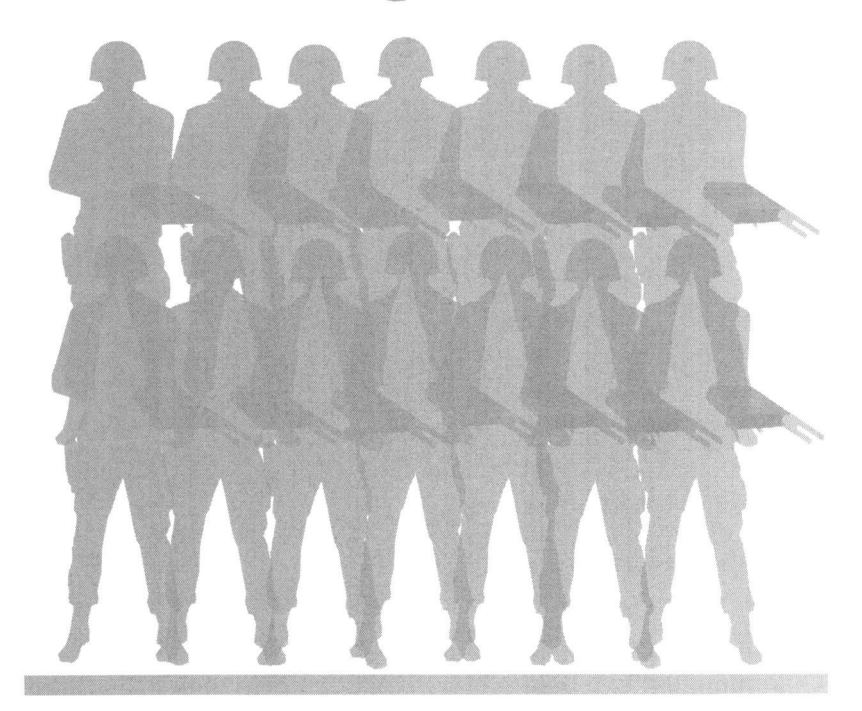

Whole Armor

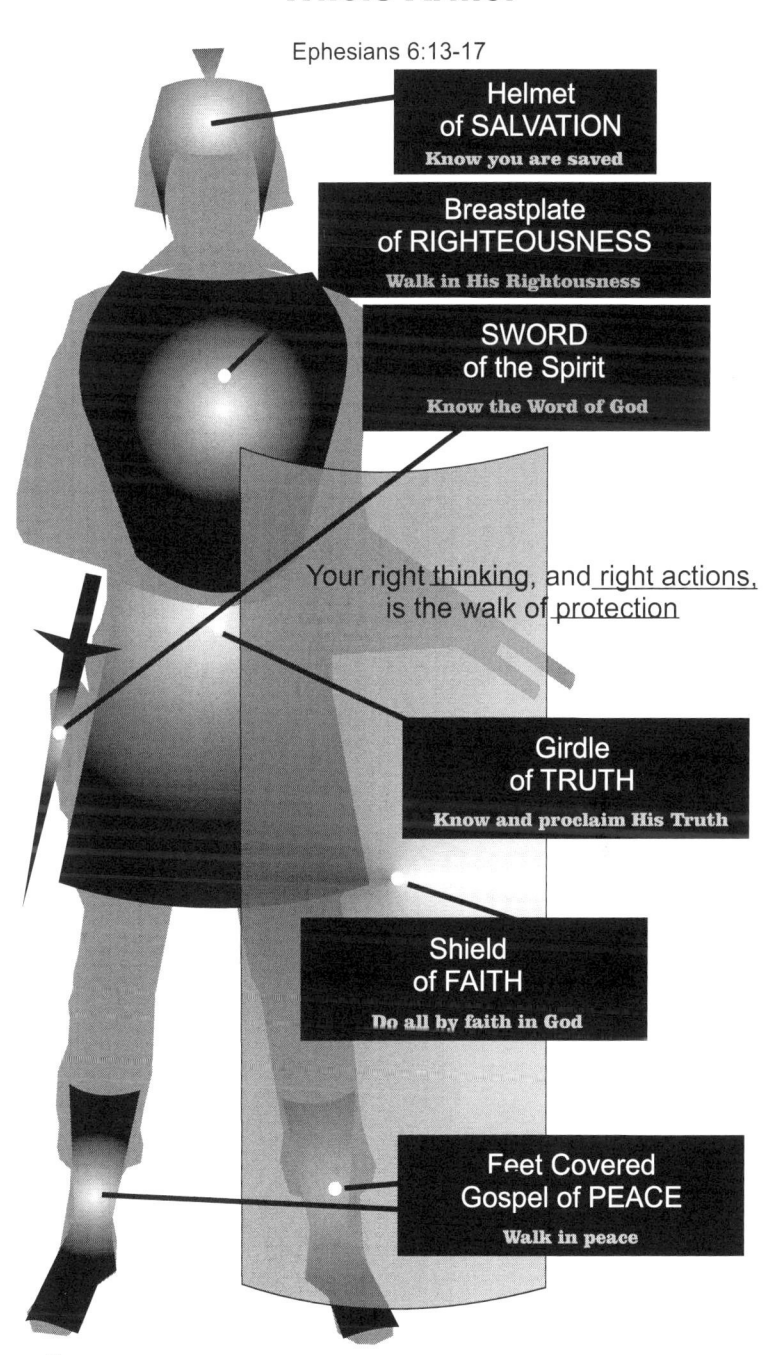

Ephesians 6:13-17

Helmet of SALVATION
Know you are saved

Breastplate of RIGHTEOUSNESS
Walk in His Righteousness

SWORD of the Spirit
Know the Word of God

Your right <u>thinking</u>, and <u>right actions</u>, is the walk of <u>protection</u>

Girdle of TRUTH
Know and proclaim His Truth

Shield of FAITH
Do all by faith in God

Feet Covered Gospel of PEACE
Walk in peace

© G. Wayne Parker

Diagram B

"Dress right dress"
Look right into God's Word to be in line and in order!

Put on the whole armour of God, that ye may be able to stand against the wiles of the devil. Ephesians 6:11

GOD'S ARMY

CHAPTER XI
Weapons

A WORD OF KNOWLEDGE

"If you really want to shatter the efforts of the enemy show him blessed quietness."

Weapons

A weapon in the case of war is a fighting instrument. It is used to help defeat the enemy. In previous chapters we have made it clear that our warfare is of a spiritual nature. Therefore, if we are to be successful in battle our weaponry must be spiritual. While a regular army is equipped with material weapons such as guns, planes, and battleships, we have weapons of much greater power. First of all, we are equipped with the power of the Almighty God. Just think about that! The all powerful, the one who it is impossible to defeat, is for us! What a powerful position in war. God in the person of the Holy Spirit is not only for us He is with us. The Holy Spirit has an active duty station inside of us. If that's not good enough listen to this, He has promised that He will never leave us or forsake us. Read these scriptures to confirm the above statement (2 Corinthians 10:4,5; Matthew 28:18; Hebrews 13:5). When we are under attack, we must remember how God has armed us with such tremendous spiritual power. We have the power, and authority to cast off enemy attacks, to cast down thoughts, and vain imaginations, cast out demons, and to move mountains. Yes! We can do all this and more in Christ through the Holy Spirit.

We mentioned that the mind is the main field of battle. Like missiles, ungodly thoughts are aimed at our minds. These missiles are fired towards us, but if we are on guard duty, we can counter with the power missiles of the Holy Spirit (THE WORD OF GOD), that is in our new minds. Yes, blast them out of the air before they explode in our heads. "Soldier, shoot back!"

"Fight back!" Use that awesome power within you. Speak to your circumstances, it's all warfare (Mark 11:23). Shoot back with your words of faith. Fire back at that old enemy, X it out of your mind, reject it, send it to file 13, the trash bin. These are all strategies we can use to counter on the attacks of the mind (Read 1 Timothy 1:18). "Soldier! You know who you are, you know what you now have." Our Commander has given us orders. He tells us to fight , and don't be afraid. (2 Timothy 1:7).

Our faith in God's Holy Word is more powerful than anything our enemies can launch against us. When we by faith activate God's word we are making the stand we have been called to make. We are soldiers, we stand in there, we don't hang in there. Hanging is a bad position. Stand on in there! Read (Ephesians 6:13,14). We have been given power to win, arm yourself with God's Word. "Use your weapon soldier!" (Luke 10:19; Acts 1:8). In the book of Revelation we see Jesus coming back to do away with evil. His weapon will not be an atomic bomb, the weapon He will use is His mouth. We can do the same now as His soldiers.

Remember along with our uniform came the SWORD OF THE SPIRIT. Weaponry is a part of our uniform of defense and attack. The sword of the Spirit is the Word of God. In Revelation Chapter 19 the sword of His mouth will be used to destroy the enemy. The sword of His mouth is His Word, we have His Word now, let's use it soldier. Read (Revelation 19:15-21), God's Word is our weapon!

Remember this soldier : we are equipped with awesome power, and this power is not only to fight the evils of this world. We are to use our weapons to help bring many others into God's Kingdom. <u>HIS WORD</u>, <u>FAITH</u>, <u>PRAYER</u>, <u>AN OBEDIENT LIFE IN CHRIST</u>, these are all our weapons. Fight on soldier, fight good soldier. Fight, Fight, Fight, WE WIN!

"Use your weapon soldier!"

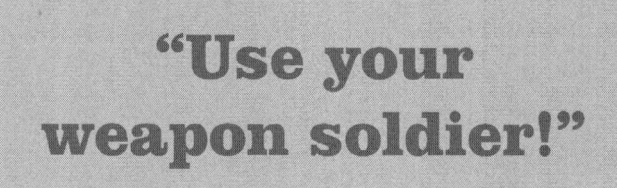

And take the helmet of salvation, and the sword of the Spirit, which is the word of God: Ephesians 6:17

GOD'S ARMY

CHAPTER XII

Job Assignment

A WORD OF KNOWLEDGE

"Give God that moment before the movement."

"Your success will not arrive based on where you want to go, it will arrive based on where He wants you to go."

Job Assignment

Most new converts are naturally curious about how God is going to use them in their Christian walk. The truth, however, is that when a soldier has been recruited the initial training is to produce a disciplined fighter. The fact is, it is only after combat training that he or she receives their job assignment. All Christians must realize that we all are called to take a fighting stance, or position. God wants all of His soldiers to be expert fighters. Even if you were not much of a fighter in your worldly setting, you must learn the divine methods for spiritual warfare.

As Christians, we must be trained to take a vigilant stance in order to be victorious here on earth. Although our spirits have been sealed, and cannot be touched by Satan, we are called to a mental battle ground. God wants us to train for mental warfare by casting down imaginations, and every high thing that exalts itself against the knowledge of God, and bringing into captivity every thought to the obedience of Christ; (2 Corinthians 10:5). Yes, the mind is our battle ground in spiritual warfare! Notice, that verse brings out the fact that we must guard our minds against that which attempts to degrade the knowledge of God.

The knowledge of God is His Word. We must be trained in His Word in order to guard against the ungodly thoughts that will attack us there. The mind is (the war zone). The Christian fight is now more mental, not physical. In our mental realm there is the constant need for battle. That's right! Our spiritual warfare is fought in our minds. The enemy attacks us there to rob us of our blessings. So, it is there we must stand and fight on a daily basis.

The weapons we use to fight are mostly invisible. We are to fight from the Holy Spirit, to our spirit, and from our spirit, we download to our minds. The weapons of the spirit realm are much greater than the physical, carnal realm (2 Corinthians 10:4). As Christian soldiers it is our call, and duty to fight. We are in a good fight of faith (2 Timothy 6:12). There must be a constant daily fight against all that is ungodly. Each day we war against the negative thoughts that attempt to govern our walk in this earth. Thoughts that want to turn our bodies to move in ungodliness. So learning to fight should be our first priority after salvation. Before we seek our spiritual job assignments, we should be trained to be warriors, fighting soldiers. After a regular soldier has been trained to fight, he or she is then given training for their support assignment. The same pattern should be exercised in the Army of the Lord. After the soldier gains fighting knowledge and is armed, they are ready for spiritual warfare (attacks on the mind).

After completing boot camp or basic training the soldier is then required to train and work in other areas. They are assigned jobs that will support the army as a whole. For instance, in the regular army there are areas of support such as engineering, maintenance, supply, administration, cooks, drill instructors, etc. God's Army is the same. The Bible refers to these support jobs or assignments as spiritual gifts. Every believer has a gift that is to support the kingdom work of God. Some believers may have more than the one gift.

Be sure you read 1 Corinthians 12:4-11 which lists many of these gifts. In the body of Christ every gift should be used on behalf of the entire body. We are fitly joined together and each body member should be a support. You might also want to read Romans 12:3-5 to confirm this.

Now comes this question, what is my support assignment or the gift God has blessed me with? This is the question most new Christians have in mind. Lord what area would you have me work in? What do you want me to do Lord? Do you want me to preach or what? Then you have others who don't ask God, they tell Him what they are good at doing. They assume that they are good in a certain area and should be placed there. They think their job assignment will be in the area they feel most comfortable. In other words, they think they will do well in certain areas so they pursue it. They don't seek orders from God they just start working based on their own thoughts. They don't know any better, but they are really moving in an unharnessed zeal. They think they are doing the right thing. This type of movement should not happen.

So how is it we get to know what God is assigning us? Here again the subject of lordship must be brought to light. Are we the ones calling the shots or are we allowing God to assign His will to us? It is God who should be assigning us to places He has ordained for us before the foundation of the world. Let God lead you, He knows what He's doing, we don't.

In Proverbs 3:5, the Word of God tells us that we are to trust in the Lord, and not our own thinking. We are to allow Him to lead us in all our endeavors. Psalm 37:23 tells the believer that their steps should be ordered by the Lord. As soldiers we must wait for orders first.

Although this may seem elementary, the fact is we really don't know what we are doing without God. We make assumptions and many times find ourselves in a wilderness of quandary simply because we ignore or disregard the personal direction of the almighty God. One day I remember standing in front of the mirror and the voice of God said "you are stupid without Jesus." Say it! Say, "I am stupid without Jesus." Even though my spirit knew it to be truth, my old mind did not want to admit it. Out of my spirit I said it. "I am stupid without Jesus." For many years that became one of my God given expressions. One day after continually walking in that truth God spoke to me and said ,... "YOU ARE STUPID WITHOUT ME, BUT YOU ARE BRILLIANT WITH ME," Amen!

God knows where he wants to take us as His children and soldiers. He has planned special duty assignments for all of us. He has placed special gifts within us. These gifts are waiting to be launched for service in His time. These are spiritual gifts (support job assignments). Romans 11:29 reveals the fact that we have gifts and callings. We have been invited without regret to special areas of operation and service in God's army. Hopefully you read

1 Corinthians chapter 12 which tells us that there are many gifts given by the Spirit as He wills. We do not chose what our gifts are. So as obedient servants, and soldiers of God we must march to the beat of His drum. In other words, we must humble our lives to receive orders from Him. If we yield our will unto Him in LORDSHIP, He will usher us into our specialties of Christian service for Him.

Since our God is the one who has blessed us with our gifts, He is the one who knows how He wants to use us, and we are to wait on His timing and direction. When a soldier is in boot camp or basic training he or she may be assigned to help around the base camp. Let the Holy Spirit lead you everyday. Do what He tells you to do. What he tells you to do is what you then know to do, at that time of service. Do this daily, and before you know it God will have walked you into your called assignment. Here is a simple key to remember, Do what you know to do today and He will lead you to your tomorrow. If we obey Him, each day each step moves us closer to that divine place we were so curious to know. In the natural army soldiers are tested so that they are properly placed in their field of work. In God's Army however, the test is a test of obedience. Walk with Him where you are, and He will take you where He wants you to go. Obey God! You will know its right when you get there, but you must learn how to fight first. Warrior first, then support job.

Do what He tells you to do!

And why call ye me, Lord, Lord, and do not the things which I say? Luke 6:46

GOD'S ARMY

CHAPTER XIII
Duty Station

13

A WORD OF KNOWLEDGE

"Don't let the opinions of others move you. Your success in God will be based on how He moves you."

Duty Station

Now that we have an understanding of our God given job assignment areas (gifts of the spirit), lets take a look at the matter of being assigned a duty station. In the regular army following boot camp training, the soldier is then sent either to school or to a base camp (a duty station). The duty station for the Christian soldier is called the local church. Why the church? Why was the church designed? How is the church suppose to operate? In Matthew 16:18, our Lord and Savior Jesus Christ speaks of the church. A church He would build. In Ephesians 5:23 the Word says Jesus Christ is the head of the church. Yes, the head of the church. He is the Commander, and Chief of this army. Jesus Christ is the source of our directives via the Holy Spirit. When a soldier is given orders for assignment they are to come from the top, head-quarters. No soldier is to determine on their own where he or she is to be placed for duty. Moving on without orders is to be out of godly order.

Many Christians have made the mistake of assigning them selves a duty station. Some place themselves with the traditional family church. Some join the nearest church. Others assign themselves to home, and they may visit the local assembly now and then. The important question is; Did you seek the Lord for your duty station? Yes, or no? The word church in the Greek language is *ekklesia,* it's an assembly of called out people of faith in Jesus Christ. We are called out from the world, called to God, called to go forth in the Lord operating in the gifts. We should be sent to a designated duty station. The church for the soldier is his or her place for assembly and work assignment. There are some who unfortunately see the church only as a gathering for prayer, praise, and worship. The function of the church is that, and much more. The church is to be a training camp, a work station, a spiritual hospital for wounded soldiers, and a office that monitors God's rules of righteousness. The church should be a base camp that offers to meet the needs of the Christian soldier from start to finish. The church must be the place that clearly raises the standards of Jesus Christ, so that every soldier reaches his / her greatest potential. Just as there is need for correction and discipline in the natural army so it is in church . Read the following scriptures, (Matthew 18:15-17; 1 Corinthians 6:1,2).

Every local church should be an organized site set to operate in a godly way. This takes us to the matter of offices or positions of authority held in the church. God is a God of order not confusion. He appoints and sets in place certain soldiers in lead positions of service. Notice we said He sets in place. God's places of leadership are by Divine calling, not by self-appointment or other ungodly entrances. When God establishes, He equips for action. Read 1 Corinthians 12:28-29, and also Ephesians 4:11-12 for clarity, and confirmation.

When God sets a soldier as a pastor / bishop type, they are to follow the charge and directives of the Holy Spirit, and they should not be abusing or making merchandise of what belongs to God. Pastors are set to teach and care for the sheep not abuse them. Read Acts 20:28, and 1Peter 5:2-4 for more scriptural insight.

Make certain you have sought the Lord for your church, (your duty station). Trust in the Lord with all your heart, and lean not unto your own understanding in <u>all</u> your ways acknowledge Him, and He will direct your path, (Proverbs 3:5,6). God knows how He wants to use us and where He wants to use us. In the regular army soldiers are assigned based on their skills, and where the skill is needed. If your skill is needed, and head-quarters sees fit to send you, your orders are cut for reassignment.

If the Army of God ran in that fashion each local church would be supplied every gift necessary for base operation. How sad it is if a given base is lacking in godly function because the ones that should be assigned there are some place of their own choosing. I hear someone asking this question. How do I get personal orders of assignment, how will I know for sure that it is God, and not my own thinking? That's a good question, and here is your answer. If a Christian is walking in the spirit, meaning they have relinquished their will to the Lord, the Spirit of God will somehow speak to your spirit in an undeniable way. If you are sincere in following the will of God, He will not play games, or leave you hanging. Ask in sincerity and your God will answer you with clarity. Obey Him, if He reassigns you, enjoy your new God given assignment. Remain open to His will for you.

Actually the true church is an organism of true believers. The buildings we call churches are actually facilities for assembling our selves in an organized manner. The local is simply a base camp for soldiers. It is the place we go to for corporate order, worship, and fellowship. We are to be in proper order and fellowship, otherwise we will be AWOL, absent with-out leave. We all need this place, we need each other, it is there we get to know each other.

As Christian brothers and sisters, soldiers of the Lord, we are called to assemble ourselves in unity. We are one body, one army. Where ever you may happen to be assigned, make sure you are fighting the good fight, and not one of your fellow soldiers in the Lord. Our assemblies are to be places of love, unity, and edification. Be expert in your aim of love. Love is our badge of service unto the Lord. Read this, Hebrews 10:23-25. Let's make the best of this God given tour of duty.

GOD'S ARMY

CHAPTER XIV

Tour of Duty

14

A WORD OF KNOWLEDGE

"Only God can lead you to what is best for you. Let Him be your tour guide."

Tour Of Duty

The tour of duty in any branch of the armed forces is the amount of time the soldier serves his or her country. The tour of duty usually lasts from two to four years. The time may differ depending on the branch of service. Once the service person finishes their time in service, then there is a discharge from army duties. If the soldier has done well he/she is given an honorable discharge. Those who choose making a career of the service are sometimes called "lifers." This is how every Christian should be described. We as born again Christians are LIFERS. When we join God's Army we receive the promise of life eternal. Life that will never cease, life without breech, break, or any interval.

Think of the security soldiers have when they can go off to battle knowing that at the end of the war they win and that they will never die. Read what Jesus says in (St. John 11:25-26). That scripture is telling us that in the spirit, the true essence of our tripartite being, we are protected from death. As we war against our enemies, we do not have to fear death. Read what it says in (1 John 2:25). Eternal life is a promise from God, what an awesome blessing of God.

When a soldier joins the regular army they are on duty 24/7. They are always on call. So it is in the Christian army. We are to constantly be on guard against the world the flesh, and the Devil. There will come a time when our tour of duty in this earth will be over, but in the mean time we are to fight. Until we leave this tour of duty we are to fight. Every day we are to stand and battle. Not physical, but a mental / spiritual warfare. We can fight boldly without fear of death.

The very reason God has left us down here after salvation is to fight. By the power of the Holy Spirit, God wants us to make a mockery of the enemy. God wants to use us in kingdom building; helping Him bring others out of spiritual darkness. As lights of God, we fight to win others to the kingdom of light. It is God's desire to use us in a way that will put His enemies to shame; however this fruitfulness can only be accomplished by our obedience to the Holy Spirit. When we march to the cadence of the Spirit, we produce the fruit of the Spirit. When we operate in the Spirit, we are then demonstrating the likeness of Christ. As God's Army we have been given power over the enemy. When our Lord and Savior rose from the dead, He proclaimed all power had been given to Him. In other words, He striped Satan of his illegal power. Read (Matthew 28:18).

In the new testament Jesus Christ gives authority to the Church to war and win against the powers of darkness. Read what the Word says in (Mark 6:7; Luke 10:19) and (Ephesians 1:19-23). Although we have been given this power, we must be warned of the fact that walking out of the fellowship of the Holy Spirit, or simply put, moving in disobedience such as being unforgiving gives Satan an advantage. Read (2 Corinthians 2:10,11). If we as soldiers don't walk in proper fellowship through obedience, the Holy Spirit becomes grieved and will stop His flow of joy and peace to our minds. Being one of God's soldiers in warfare, but existing without the blessing of His peace is a miserable state of being. It feels like you are in a dark spiritual prison.

To walk honorably before our God is to maintain a sound mind and avoid those things that we know are not pleasing to Him. (2 Timothy 2:4) says, "No man that is at war gets themselves entangled with the things of this life so that he is able to please God who has chosen him to be a soldier." That verse is telling us we have a requirement to live a practical sanctified life. The clean living of a born again believer is a righteous choice. We must chose to be on the outside, who we truly are on the inside. It is with the will we make manifest the new man created in Christ.

The positional sanctification we are blessed to have in the Spirit came by the work Jesus Christ provided on the cross; however, the practical sanctification is when we, by faith, submit to the Lordship of Jesus Christ being filled with the Holy Spirit. We should be honorable soldiers. Taking the conqueror's stance by the power of the Holy Spirit. We are to put our foot on the neck of the enemy and declare the victory the Lord has given us. We are more than conquerors through him that loved us (Romans 8:37).

When our tour of duty here on earth is finished, God will call us home. The true soldier of Jesus Christ will endure hardness as a good soldier (2 Timothy 2:3). The true soldier one who has been truly born again will go to the end, and our God promises to never leave us or forsake us. God is with us, and if God be for us who can (win) against us. Read what it says in (Hebrews 13:5;) and (Romans 8:31). If we as children of God want to walk this earth in victory, we must be militant minded. That is, we are to be lovingly militant minded, with our minds renewed for war.

Think like a soldier, act like a soldier, stand like you are a soldier, and fight like you are a soldier, because you are a soldier. At the end of your tour of duty here, proclaim as did Paul; " I have fought a good fight I have finished my course". Soldier be encouraged. I hope this training has enlightened you to a mind set of victory. You are on the winning team. Keep fighting that good fight. Some day soon The Lord of Host, The Lord of Battle will come to relieve us of duty and take us home. He will then give us R and R. In the regular army its rest and recuperation. For the church THE ARMY OF GOD it will be a RAPTURE and REIGN with Him. God bless you, and keep fighting good because our God loves to see us in a GOOD FIGHT.

Fight Good, Our Savior And Lord Is Coming Soon !

GOD'S ARMY

Biblical Glossary Of Fighting Words

GOD'S ARMY

"Operating in God's Word is what will unify us, stabilize us, and empower us in warfare."

A Biblical Glossary

Armies..........Re. 19:14
Armour.........Ep. 6:11
Armour.........Ep. 6:13
Armour.........2 Cor. 6:7
Armour.........Rom. 13:12
Armoury.......Jer. 50:25
Army............Re. 19:19
Arrow............Ps. 11:2
Arrow............Ps. 91:5
Assigned......Jos. 20:8
Battle............Ps.18:39
Battle............Ps. 24:8
Battle............Ps. 55:18
Battle............Ps. 147:7
Buckler.........Ps. 18:2
Buckler.........Pr.. 2:7
Buckler.........Song 4:4
Captain........Heb. 2:10
Captive........2 Tim. 2:25,26
Captive........2 Tim. 3:6
Captivity.......Ps. 126:1-4
Command..Jer. !:7
Commanded..Jer.11:4
Conduct......1 Cor 16:11
Conquerors..Rom. 8:37
Defence.......Ps. 7:10
Defence.......Ps. 59:16,17
Defence.......Phil. 1:17
Defenced ...,Jer. 1: 17,18
Defend.........Ps. 59:1
Defendest.....Ps.5:11
Deliver...........Ps. 31:15
Deliver..........Rom. 7:24
Deliver..........Gal. 1:4
Deliver..........2 Tim. 4: 17,18
Deliver..........Heb. 2:15
Deliver..........2 Pet. 2:9
Deliverance..Lk. 4:18

Delivered......Ps. 56:13
Delivered......Prov. 11:8
Encamp.......Ps. 27:3
Encampeth..Ps. 34:7
Enemies.......Ps. 6:10
Enemies.......Ps. 18:3
Enemies.......41:5
Enemies.......119:157
Enemies.......Prov. 16:7
Enemy.........Ps. 143:9
Enemy.........Ps. 8:2
Enemy.........Ps. 64:1
Enemy.........Prov. 27:6
Enemy.........Is. 59:19
Enemy.........Matt.13:28
Enemy.........Lk. 10:19
Fight............Ps. 35:1
Fight............Ps. 56:2
Fight............1 Cor. 9:26
Fight............1 Tim. 6:12
Fight.........Heb. 10:32
Fortress.....Ps. 18:2
Fortress.....Ps. 31:3
Foes.........Prov. 27:6
Foes.........Matt. 10:36
Force.......Matt. 11:12
Fought.....Ps. 109:3
Fought.....1 Cor. 15:32
Fought.....2 Tim. 4:7
Garrisons.1 Chr. 18:13
Gate........Ps. 127:5
Gates.......Ps. 146:13
Gates.......Matt. 16:18
General....1 Chr. 27:34
Gird..........1 Pet. 1:13
Girded......Ps. 18:39

A Biblical Glossary (Cont.)

Girded......Lk. 12:35
Girdeth.....Ps. 18:32
Guard.......2 Sam. 23:23
Guide.......Ps. 32:8
Guide.......Ps. 48:14
Guide.......Lk. 1:79
Guide.......St. Jn. 16:13
Guided.....Ps. 78:52
Guided.....Ps. 78:72
Helmet......Eph. 6:17
Helmet......1 Thess. 5:8
Host...........Ps. 27:3
Host...........Ps. 136:15
Hosts................Ps. 46:7
March..............Ps. 68:7
March..............Hab. 3:12,13
Obedience......1 Cor. 1o:5,6
Obedience......Heb. 5:8
Obedient.........2 Cor. 2:9
Obey...............1 Sam. 15:22
Obey...............Act. 5:29
Obey...............Heb. 5:9
Obeying..........Jug. 2:17
Occupy...........Lk. 19:13
Officers............Josh. 1:10
Order...............Ps. 119:33
Ordered...........Ps. 37:23
Posts................Prov. 8:34
Promote...........Prov. 4:8
Promotion........Ps. 75: 6,7
Rank................Num. 2:16
Ranks..............Mk. 6:40
Report.............Prov. 15: 30
Report.............Jn. 12:38
Rereward.........Josh. 6:9;

Salute.........Rom. 16:16
Salute.........Heb. 13:24
Saluted.......Acts 18:22
Secret.........Ps. 25:14;
　　　　　　Prov. 3:32
Secrets.......Prov. 11:13
Serve..........Ps. 2:11
Serve.........Ps. 100:2
Service......Rom. 12:1
Service......Heb. 9:6
Shield........Ps. 28:7;
Shield........Ps. 33:20
Shield........Eph. 6:16
Soldier.......Phil. 21:25
Soldier.......2 Tim. 2:3,4
Spear........Ps. 46:9
Spy............Num. 13:16,17
Spy............Gal. 2:4
Stand........Eph. 6:11-14
Subdue.....Ps. 47:3
Subdued...Ps. 81:14
Subdued...Heb. 11:33
Supply.......Phil. 4:19
Sword.......Eph. 6:17
Teach.......1 Tim. 4:11
Teachers...Eph. 4:11
Tower.........Ps. 18:2
Tower.........Ps. 61:3
Tower.........Ps. 144:2
Trained......Gen. 14:14
Traitors.......2 Tim. 3:4
Tread.........Ps. 60:12
Tread.........Lk. 10:19
Triumph.....Ps. 41:11
Triumph.....2 Cor. 2:14
Trodden.....Ps. 119:118
Troop.........Ps. 18:29

A Biblical Glossary (Cont.)

Troop.........Ps. 9:6
Victory.......Ps. 98:1
Victory.......1 Jn. 5:4
Walls..........Prov. 25:28
Walls..........Heb. 11:30
War............Ps. 27:3

War............Ps. 144:1
Warfare.....2 Cor. 10:4
Warfare.....1 Tim. 1:18
Warreth......2 Tim. 2:4
Warring......Rom. 7:23

Boots On The Ground Soldier!

If You Are A True Christian
You Are A Soldier
In God's Army.
If You Are A True
Pastor/Teacher
(Drill Instructor)
Teach Them How
To Fight.
(BOOT CAMP)

Lets Make A
Mockery
Of The Enemy.

Its War Time Now!

Heaven Comes Later!

&

WE WIN BIG TIME!